Welco
Chil
to Communion

by

Daniel Young

Chaplain of Dean Close School, Cheltenham

'Welcome one another, therefore, as Christ has welcomed you, for the glory of God.' (Rom. 15.7)

GROVE BOOKS

BRAMCOTE NOTTS. NG9 3DS

CONTENTS

ACKNOWLEDGEMENTS

—to Michael Vasey, who as a tutor first encouraged me to look at Ely and all that; next inspired an interest in 'Family Festivals'; and finally suggested the idea of this booklet;

—to Barry Miller, of the Church of England Board of Education, who literally went out of his way to meet me and to provide much of the documentary evidence on which this booklet is based;

—to Colin Buchanan, for unfailing stimulus and patience;

—to the rest of the Board of Education working party for organizing a most helpful 'consultation';

—to the parish of Bushbury, where I learned how firm discipline can be combined with genuine welcome;

—to the school whose chaplain I have just become, making it clear that neither they nor any of the above are responsible for the views which I express herein;

—and finally, to my wife, Sue, and our children Joanna and Kathryn.

First Impression July 1983

ISSN 0144–1728

ISBN 0 907536 50 6

INTRODUCTION

It would be interesting to conduct a poll of first reactions to the title of this booklet: 'Welcoming children to communion.' How many readers immediately envisage what we envisage: tiny children, even babes in arms, actually receiving bread and wine with their parents; not to mention older, but also still unconfirmed, children, part of the family of God, sharing in the family meal? It is a fact, as we shall see, that in increasing numbers English parishes are moving forward towards this goal; and to those involved with this movement there will be little that is new in this booklet, though I hope there will be real encouragement. But we must realize that this 'alternative practice', as it is coming to be known, has not as yet penetrated very far into the traditional consciousness of the Church of England. It may be, indeed we believe wholeheartedly that it *is,* an idea whose time has come; but for those for whom it is a *new* idea, this booklet begins with four basic principles upon which to base the practice. I hope I have taken seriously the misgivings people actually have, and if nothing else, that what I say will indicate the need for deeper theological work in the whole area of Christian nurture. Only the whole truth into which the Spirit is leading us will save us from two pitfalls. On the one hand there is the pitfall of sentimentality about children, which would lead us to welcome them to communion on inadequate or spurious grounds so that we would then fail to encourage growth in true faith. On the other hand there is the pitfall of Pharisaism (which is a danger to us all); Pharisaism exalts man-made rules and scruples to the exclusion of people from the kingdom of God.

The second part of this booklet, 'Practical Questions', will I trust be of value to all who have taken the first part seriously. So many questions come to mind when we contemplate so radical a departure from tradition as the welcoming of children to communion. Of course, it is only a departure from our particular tradition; the excursus on church history should make that clear. But it does have implications that spread out very wide indeed across the life of our churches. Here it would be so valuable to hear from those who have tackled some of those implications first hand. I hope that sooner or later opportunities will be established in the dioceses for the discussion of these issues; but meanwhile, perhaps the odd letter to *News of Liturgy . . .*?

1. BASIC PRINCIPLES

(i) The priority of grace

This is the place to begin. The verse from Romans 15[1] which I have chosen as an epigraph states the principle: our response is *preceded* by God's grace in Christ. So often in the New Testament this is tellingly expressed: 'in this is love, not that we loved God but that he loved us and sent his Son . . .'; '. . . while we were yet helpless . . . while we were yet sinners . . .'; '. . . you have not chosen me, but I have chosen you . . .' How hard it is to live with and to dwell upon these statements of the absolute and unconditional nature of God's grace: it is too easy to step in with our own conditions, either for ourselves or for others. But we must say it again: it is not that God's grace is called forth in response to our faith; our faith is called forth in response to God's grace. And yet we deny the sacramental 'means of grace' to children until they show (in our judgment) a response of faith. In our eucharistic discipline we are so frequently denying the priority of God's grace. To admit children would not, on the other hand, be to deny the necessity of faith in them: that point is dealt with later. It would be to involve our children in an experience of God's grace in Christ which would make a vital contribution in calling forth faith. We know how God in Christ has welcomed us, and in so welcoming us has called forth faith and love in response. How can we not also welcome others in that way, children included?

(ii) **Children** *can* **'discern the body'. (I Cor. 11.29)**

We know that Jesus welcomed children; we know that he made childlikeness a condition for entry into the Kingdom; we know that he thanked his Father for revealing to babes what had been hidden from the wise and understanding. We must not dissolve the force of all this by treating these references to children metaphorically. Their import is underlined by the incarnation: Jesus was born, and lived and grew, as a true child; and at every stage: '. . . in him all the fulness of God was pleased to dwell.' (Col. 1.19). It is not that as a tiny baby Jesus was imperfect, and gradually grew to perfection: it is that at each stage he was fully himself, though developing and learning by experience as we all do, and limited as everyone is limited through all the stages of human life. So childhood is revalued, not only in the Gospels, but also in the person of Christ himself: it is not a state of formlessness out of which something worthwhile must in time be made, but a stage of development with its own value and significance. These rudimentary theological reflections on the nature of childhood are reinforced by the discoveries of modern education theory. Children are in relationship with their human environment from before birth, not only biologically but also socially and psychologically; and the very earliest experiences are 'understood' in the sense that they are assimilated and formative of future learning and behaviour. It is believed by many experts now that the pregnant woman passes on to her unborn child her own feelings

[1] Romans 15.7. This verse is an interesting summary of the argument in chapter 14 about food and drink and the observance of 'days', in the course of which is established *both* the principle of freedom in Christ *and* consideration for the scruples of others. The principle I am establishing above; the scruples I will consider later. The verse is set out on the title-page.

about her situation; the actual circumstances of birth are increasingly felt to play a crucial role in later development; and early experiences of security or insecurity are well known to affect the stability of the person later on. As the child develops, successive stages in the understanding of experience have been noted; and although these are not so clearcut as was supposed, it is beyond dispute that even very young children absorb the meaning which underlies concrete symbols, even if they cannot conceptualize that meaning until much later. Rejection or acceptance; participation or alienation: these are sophisticated *concepts,* but the *experiences* underlying them are the alternatives which face our children as we decide whether to welcome them to communion or not. As the title of this section shows, I am well aware of the hesitations people have based on I Corinthians 11.27ff; and it is quite right that we should focus attention on that *locus classicus* concerning eucharistic discipline. If I am right, there are two aspects to Paul's warning about 'discerning the body': cognitive and moral. The cognitive aspect is a simple failure to grasp something of the significance of this common meal: 'When you meet together it is not the Lord's Supper that you eat.' The moral aspect in the case of the Corinthians is the wilful offence involved: '. . . do you despise the church of God and humiliate those who have nothing?' In making the Lord's Supper an individual self-indulgence, at the expense of others, the Corinthians have both cognitively and morally failed to discern the body: and the 'body' must represent in some way both the significance of what is consumed and the significance of the community who consume it. 'It' is the indivisible body of Christ. Can children discern this body? Cognitively, the answer must be 'yes', because as shown above we know the experience to be profoundly accessible to them, the experience of acceptance and participation in the body of Christ as, together with the immediate fellowship of their own family, and the wider fellowship of the family of God, they share in bread and wine. Even very tiny children recognize a special meal; they can therefore appreciate some special significance about this bread and this cup in the context of the celebration as a whole, though the conceptual content of that significance comes to them only gradually as they grow[1] (and have any of those who read these lines fully grasped it?) in the community which expresses the life of Christ made available on the cross and celebrated at each communion. Morally, what is required is that children should be able to discern the body in proportion to their capacity for sinning against it.[2] Now whatever our interpretation of the doctrine of original sin, it is certain that even very young children can be sinners! However, it is hard to imagine them sinning against the body of Christ in the Corinthian manner, despising the church of God and humiliating those who have nothing. Therefore their rudimentary grasp of the significance of that body is in proportion with their small capacity to sin against it. It is we adults who need to heed Paul's warnings—especially if we are in doubt as to welcoming children to communion.

[1] Not to mention those whose participation in communion will ever be child-like, notably the mentally handicapped. Those who have had the privilege of belonging to the same fellowship as one of these 'little ones' will know that they can 'discern the body' all right: they give and receive love with a freedom we have lost.

[2] I owe this observation to Colin Buchanan.

(iii) The unity of the sacraments

There is still a variety of approach to the sacraments within the Church of England; but most would find acceptable the statement that baptism is sacramental initiation into life in Christ, and the eucharist is the continuing celebration of that life, made available at Calvary. (Any questions apparently begged by this formulation will be addressed in the 'Practical questions' later.) For the moment, it is enough to note that in both the prayer book (1662) and the ASB we are claiming regeneration, or new birth, or life in Christ, or however we describe it, *for the infant* whom we are baptizing. We can only circumvent this by dividing baptism into two kinds: adult baptism which is accompanied by faith, and infant baptism which is followed, considerably later, by faith as expressed in confirmation. But this division involves undermining the priority of God's grace in baptism, misunderstanding the nature of faith (see above for both these points) and creating two different doctrines for the one baptism. No; if we believe in infant baptism at all, we must believe it has exactly the same significance as adult baptism.[1] And if the child has been buried with Christ by baptism into death, and now shares that newness of life of which St. Paul goes on to speak in Romans chapter six, how can we withhold from him or her the sacrament which is corporate reappropriation of that Life? Moreover, in baptism we have welcomed the infant as a fellow-member of the body of Christ; how can we fail to welcome him or her to communion, when we say:

> 'Though we are many, we are one body,
> for we all share in one bread.'

We dare not then proceed to divide the members of that body into communicant and non-communicant, largely on the grounds of age. That would be to destroy the unity of the body of Christ proclaimed both at baptism, whether of adults or of infants, and at communion. It would also be to destroy the unity of the sacraments, the very principle I have been trying to establish in this section: if we baptize infants then we ought also to communicate them.

(iv) The nature of the church

The New Testament shows quite clearly that children were a part of the church (see below); and Jesus shows that they are a gift and a model for believers (see above). Where modern churches, like the New Testament church, have a strong sense of themselves as 'the body of Christ', there tends to be increasing interest in communicating children, as would also be expected from the section on the sacraments above. Perhaps it is we who fail to 'discern the body' when we do not welcome our children to communion.

[1] Questions of baptismal discipline are discussed below.

BRIEF EXCURSUS
on the history of welcoming children to communion

What of the New Testament church? There is no mention of child communicants, true enough; nor is there mention of women communicants! Any argument from silence is precarious, but it must be said that the burden of proof lies with those who hold that children were not admitted: the New Testament makes it clear that in so many other ways children were an integral part of the church. But the time of the early Fathers the practice was established; and somewhat later in North Africa Cyprian and Augustine give the practice extensive Scriptural and theological warranty.[1] Augustine also dwelt on the nature of childhood as the ideal state for the communicant. The separation of baptism and admission to the eucharist, and medieval developments in sacramental theology, struck at the roots of the practice *in the West,* through there were interesting survivals and revivals both unreformed and reformed.[2] In the East, of course, the practice has continued since the beginning. The early twentieth century saw the Roman Catholic church admit children to communion (following confession) at seven, and there has subsequently been, as we shall see, increasing confidence in the provision for these child communicants. Various recent provision has been made in the Lutheran churches and the Presbyterian churches; great interest is being shown in the Church of Scotland (see the booklist); and in the United States, New Zealand and some dioceses in Canada, Anglicans now admit children of any age (in principle).

Much has been happening even in the Church of England. In the early seventies, interest was focussed on the Ely report on Christian Initiation, in which the chief recommendation relevant to this study was that baptism alone should be seen as the qualification for admission to communion. That seemed to be rejected by General Synod in 1976; but interest continued to grow, and in 1980 the Diocesan Religious Education and Children's Work Advisers requested the Education and Community Committee of the Board of Education to find what was happening where and how. It became clear that various experiments were taking place in parishes, and certain dioceses were showing interest; in 1981 the Winchester diocesan motion set out below first appeared on the General Synod agenda; and, in order further to monitor the situation, a small working party was set up, by the Committee mentioned above in early 1982, to be chaired by the Bishop of Knaresborough. By January 1983 the Working Party had written to all diocesan bishops, and had discovered that 18 of them had already officially permitted experiments in admission to Holy Communion prior to confirmation, and that seven of them had had their own working parties on the subject. In Southwark diocese in particular 'experimentation' was very widespread. A list of typical criteria for the

[1] See David Holeton's first essay 'The Communion of Infants and Young Children' in G. Muller-Fahrenholz (ed.) . . . *And do not hinder them.* (W.C.C., 1982).

[2] See David Holeton *Infant Communion Then and Now* (Grove Liturgical Study 27, 1981).

admission of children to communion was also compiled; and in addition to these 'official' approaches, there were dozens of responses to letters in the church press requesting information. The Winchester motion meanwhile inched its way to the head of the queue and was finally debated in General Synod on 8 February 1983 in the following form:

> 'That this Synod requests the Standing Committee to review the General Synod's Resolution of July 1976 disallowing the admission of baptized persons to the Holy Communion followed at a later stage by Confirmation, [with a view, in the light of the growing demand for such an option, to permitting the introduction of this change in certain dioceses for a period of twelve years, as a pilot experiment].'

Despite all this, General Synod was slightly cautious: an amendment was tabled to delete the part shown here in square brackets, and this was accepted by 143 votes to 124; then the amended motion was passed, by 228 votes to 104, requesting Standing Committee to review the 1976 resolution, but without the original request for a 12-year pilot experiment in certain dioceses. Nevertheless, this has been seen as encouraging further developments, both amongst the bishops and also by the Working Party. The Working Party called a preliminary conference in London in June 1983 for representatives of parishes which are following an experimental practice, and around 40 persons participated. Meanwhile, all the evidence is that in the parishes (and other Christian institutions) increasing numbers of God's family in the Church of England (as well as elsewhere) are determined to welcome children to communion. They, and now we, have answered the question 'Why?' Now for the second question.

2. PRACTICAL QUESTIONS

(i) What about initiation?

The argument above about the nature of the sacraments was meant to show that baptism and communion belong together: and the inference from that is that Christian initiation is complete in baptism. But there are those who for exegetical, historical, and theological, reasons believe that Christian initiation is baptism plus (anointing and) laying on of hands. The argument is a technical one, and I refer interested readers to the booklist, where both sides are represented. But it must be said that for both 'sides' there is at present a serious inconsistency in the ASB initiation rites. The ASB boldly arranges these to suggest that the *norm* is adult baptism followed by confirmation *and* communion, all together; whereas for infants there is provision only for baptism (and for making the sign of the cross with oil if that is seen as an 'extra'), with of course later confirmation. I hope that what I have said so far will have made it clear that whatever Christian initiation is, it cannot be separated into different components chronologically: as has been well said, you cannot partly belong to the body of Christ any more than you can be partly pregnant. So, granted that initiation is all of a piece, we have got to find a way of applying it consistently to both adults and infants. Those who see baptism as complete in itself must be allowed to apply that consistently; likewise those who would include laying on of hands as an integral part of the sacrament. Then both will be satisfied that initiation is complete, and adults and children, thus incorporated in the body of Christ, will together discern and share in that body at communion. If it is objected that for some to be simply baptizing while others are also laying on hands might lead to disunity, I would reply that whatever form initiation takes it should (as an ideal) be the bishop who presides over it. This is another important aspect to the need for consistency; the bishop is the unifying factor, who always was responsible entirely for initiation until thwarted by geography and numbers, and who should now assume again this responsibility. He will have to be adaptable; but only he can restore to initiation the significance it must be seen to have, expressed in the continuing fellowship of the Lord's Supper. Geography is no longer a problem, except that local practice of initiation may vary as indicated above; and numbers, even with the present quota of bishops, need not be a problem either, if we are prepared to be fully consistent about initiation. For if we are, and we really do see it as the gateway to communion, it will force us to face the issue of baptismal discipline.

(ii) How will it affect baptismal discipline?

If it were generally grasped that baptism leads to communion, it might make baptismal discipline more straightforward. At present, what we *say* about the significance of baptism is not matched by our *practice*. Much can be done, I know, with the rite of baptism itself: it must demonstrate the new life it proclaims, and its power and significance must be seen to be congruous with the new life that is celebrated at the eucharist. But liturgical/symbolic consistency is not enough;

baptismal discipline has to begin earlier. So, on the grounds of the unity between baptism and eucharist, I believe we have to say to parents who bring infants for baptism:

> 'If we were to baptize your child, we should also welcome him or her to communion. But we long to welcome *the whole family,* to see you all together with us round the Lord's Table; it is not right for infants to be isolated from their parents. So come and get to know God's family, week by week; and come to a series of learning groups where we discuss the new life in Christ.'

I have tried to put to it as positively as I can, because I think we often see baptismal discipline as something rather negative and harsh. Sadly, it is often received as such; what we should be saying to people is:

> 'Look, this is all about a tremendous new life. We think you would miss out if we just took your baby and baptized him/her and said goodbye. We want you all together to experience this new life, so that when we welcome your baby into it by baptism, we and you can celebrate it together at communion.'

I am firmly convinced this is what we should be looking for: whole families coming forward for admission to communion, including the baptism of those as yet unbaptized. And at such a great occasion, the presence of the bishop would be most appropriate. I know great pastoral sensitivity is needed in the case of divided families; but that does not stop us aiming at whole families as an ideal. In any case, as a principal, at least one parent should be a regular communicant if we are to baptize an infant; otherwise we once again undermine the unity of the sacraments.

(iii) What about older children?

It is a fact that in our churches there are many older children who come to church or church-related organizations, without their parents. As baptismal patterns change, increasing numbers of these are likely to be unbaptized. If they appear to be growing in the faith and committed to the fellowship[1], then the church has a responsibility to welcome them sacramentally. To my mind this must always mean baptism first. To welcome to communion before welcoming by baptism would be to devalue both sacraments and deprive the individual of formative experiences. What is needed is a couple or family who will 'sponsor' the child in question: with the approval of the whole church and of the child's natural family, these sponsors would then take responsibility for preparing the child for baptism and communion. This would involve oversight of what the child is learning in the church organizations and, just possibly, at school; enabling him or her to learn, as appropriate to age, what the sacraments mean (see below on nurture); inviting him or her to family meals and family worship at home; and sitting together at

[1] This is for the church leadership to decide, in consultation with youth leaders and the child's family. There can be no formal set of criteria because children and circumstances differ so widely. Each child must be seen individually: but regular attendance in itself is a very positive indication.

church. Above all the child concerned must feel part of the family of God; the word 'welcome' in the title of this booklet is not supposed to be a polite convention but a warm spiritual reality.

(iv) How can we help these children to grow in Christian commitment?

I do not believe there can be any certainty about this, though I do think the old infant-baptism-teenage-confirmation pattern was far *less* certain. But welcoming children to communion is an act of faith, as is infant baptism. We cannot *ensure* that they will grow up to be mature Christian disciples, precisely because they must become increasingly responsible for their own decisions. It is the Lord alone whose faithfulness is guaranteed. But, encouraged by that, there is much we can do to encourage the response of faith in those who have received the grace of God in baptism and who continue to do so with their families at the eucharist week by week. Christian nurture begins in the home; it is there that the child first sees the response of faith and love expressed. But it is also vital that family spirituality has firm links with the life of the church, the wider family of God. There will of course be constant contact with and concern for, other members of that family; and God's family needs to be interpreted in the widest possible sense. From the earliest age children need to know that they have other 'brothers and sisters', not only at St. Mary's where they go each Sunday, but in Africa and India and the Soviet Union. Liturgically, there must be correspondence between family worship at home and worship in church, not only by singing some of the same songs, but by praying some of the same prayers. The ASB is a valuable resource for the family worship at home: many of the collects could be used week by week, and the readings for Sunday could be looked at in preparation together on Saturday evening.[1]

Christian nurture in a home where all the family share in communion will also naturally focus often on the eucharist; and there are a number of publications now which set out the liturgy for children with illustrations and explanations which could well be studied and used by the whole family.[2] Then, when the church takes on some of the responsbility for the continuing nurture of these children, there will be readymade continuity with what has been done so far. To welcome children to communion will probably force a reappraisal of all our work with young people: we shall have to integrate what goes on on Sunday with what happens during the week. Indeed, Sunday morning might be 'integrated', with the general pattern of related but separate teaching according to age group (the ministry of the word) being followed by communion altogether (the ministry of the sacrament). There are a number of publications now which integrate nurture for the whole

[1] Or see Grove Worship booklet 73, *Family Festivals,* which has a lovely 'service' for Saturday family worship. This booklet is really a handbook of suggestions for linking church and family in worship.

[2] These illustrated booklets should be studied at home, and taken to church for the family to follow the service.

church; and if it is true that the eucharist makes a major, perhaps formative, contribution to Christian nurture, then it follows that nurture must not be isolated from its proper eucharistic context. Leslie Francis' book *His Spirit is with us* (see booklist) is going to be a seminal book, in that it finds the whole structure of Christian nurture in the eucharist, and works out the detailed application of this. Much of the newer 'confirmation' material is also in tune with this holistic approach to Christian nurture: not seeing it as a hurdle to be jumped in order to be admitted to communion, but as a life-long adventure in company with fellow-travellers with whom we eat. We must do all we can to help people to continue to grow spiritually; and I believe that welcoming children to communion will both challenge those who think they have arrived (things are hidden from the wise that are revealed to babes), and encourage those who feel they never will arrive—that it is not just a matter of intellectual response.

(v) At what age should children be welcomed?

What has been said above about the nature of children and the nature of the sacraments should have made it clear that in formal terms as soon as an infant is baptized, he or she should in principle be communicated. There is no sound theological or psychological reason to delay; and if the Church of England, with an eye on Rome and other Anglican provinces, goes for the age of, let us say, seven as the gateway to communion, she will find that it will not work pastorally either. In a non-authoritarian church there will be a continual tendency for the age of communicants to get younger and younger, and a tendency for any age-limit to seem more and more anomalous. We must not fudge the principle: if we baptize infants we should be ready to communicate them.

(vi) How do we introduce the practice at national and diocesan level?

Although the principle is clear, it needs to be introduced in several steps, both nationally and locally. First, General Synod must unequivocally affirm the principle, so that a firm foundation for what is already happening in eighteen dioceses is established. Then other dioceses need to be encouraged to start working out their own way forward, with reference to what has already happened. Parishes need positive help from their dioceses, for in some cases welcoming children to communion will mean radical change, especially in churches that are already heavily involved in youth work. A possible procedure could be outlined: for example, the first step could be to offer preparation for communion to ten-to-thirteen-year-olds as an alternative to confirmation (which would be delayed—see below); then that preparation could be offered to younger children and their families; and finally families could bring children to the table, not at the end of a course of instruction, but at the beginning of a lifetime of nurture.

(vii) What about confirmation?

As well as the sacramental view of confirmation, which sees it as an integral part of Christian initiation, there exists a widespread view that it is a necessary public commitment which, so to speak, ratifies the commitment that was made vicariously in baptism. There is much in this booklet to question confirmation in that sense; but there is no doubt that many feel a need for public commitment of some sort. A recent book, *Liturgy and learning through the Life-cycle,* (see booklist) suggests that there are various stages of life where a rite of passage might usefully be provided. Take our traditional confirmation away and we may need to provide a sort of farewell to childhood for those entering puberty. Perhaps more significantly the authors suggest a sort of lay ordination for those who have settled into the responsibilities of adult life, a considered statement of their Christian commitment and ministry. This is in keeping with the emphasis today on 'every-member' ministry, and should emphasize the place of the individual in the body of Christ; the place of which the individual will have been assured at communion since the earliest days of childhood.

All of this should, I believe, take place in the context of the regular renewal of baptismal vows by the whole congregation, which could take place at Easter or Pentecost; or just possibly, whenever anyone, adult or infant, is admitted to the eucharist following his or her baptism. Certainly the presence of infants at the eucharist should have the effect of keeping in front of the whole congregation the significance of their own baptism, however long ago it may have been. It was in baptism that they were incorporated into that body of Christ in which they share now at the eucharist.

(viii) How do we involve children in the service?

In a sense this is the wrong question, and is the reason why so many non-eucharistic 'family services' have been a failure in the past. Our true concern is to involve the *whole people of God.* The presence of children makes that priority clearer. It is more and more acknowledged that it is everyone who celebrates the eucharist, the body of Christ together; and as we grasp that that body really does include all ages, we have to ask ourselves whether our present worship in general, and the text of our liturgy in particular, make that possible. The main Sunday eucharist in a parish church should *not* in principle be a solely adult service; yet so much of what happens at the moment implies that it is, and that it is for rather cerebral adults at that. Musically, things are loosening up, with the recognition that there is a variety of contributions to be made, from young and old, traditional and new, skilled and semi-skilled! Then there is dance and drama, media which are accessible to all ages and abilities, and are still very much under-used in our churches. The visual arts have a big part to play: children can produce a weekly frieze to illustrate the theme that the whole congregation has been learning together or even in some cases three-dimensional models can provide striking visual aids or props. Poems and other pieces of writing may be displayed, or even read out in response to what the Lord is saying; favourite pieces of music may be played as expressive of atmosphere. Different aspects of people's weekly work may also be illustrated in this eucharistic context, Sunday by Sunday. Far more needs to be done in most places to involve people in the intercessions. The planning can involve different groups of families and their contributions. Preparation for all this should be seen as the major weekly task of the church. But however much spiritual imagination goes into it all, the danger is that the central eucharistic prayer will seem 'flat' by comparison, with little involvement just at the point where involvement should be reaching its height. Indirectly, we have something to learn from the Roman Catholic church: I say 'indirectly' because the fine 'Eucharistic prayers for children's masses' are mainly for school celebrations, and do not anyway assume that the majority present will be communicants. But the form of the three prayers shows how greater participation in the actual canon is possible. In the first, each stage of the eucharistic action is preceded by a clear abd self-explanatory introduction: the structure is thus made explicit in a way which makes possible a deeper involvement, for example in the clear link established, on either side of the words of institution, between creation and redemption. The second eucharistic prayer has, as a refrain between Sursum Corda and Sanctus, the following:

President: With Jesus we sing your praise
All: **Glory to God in the highest**
or
Hosanna in the highest

This refrain punctuates each episode of salvation-history, and really draws the celebration together. Then, after the dominical words, in the anamnesis section of the canon, the refrain is:

All: **We praise you, we bless you, we thank you.**

This contributes to the marvellous dramatic movement of the last part of the prayer which of course in the Roman canon has such a broad sweep. The chief innovation in the third eucharistic prayer for use in children's masses is that it is entirely adaptable for use at Easter, not just with proper prefaces but with extensive emphasis throughout on the resurrection as the focus for the eucharist. I hope it is clear from what I have said that none of these prayers is in any way childish, and they all incorporate the best insights of the liturgical movement, though obviously from a Roman Catholic perspective (which is not always entirely ours). They are prayers that the whole family of God could use, in which the concerns of worship and nurture are fused in eucharistic celebration (I gather they have been recently authorized for use on a monthly basis in parish churches of the Roman communion). I am not advocating their use in Anglican situations, nor am I saying that we should produce our own 'Eucharistic prayers for children'. But I am arguing for maximum involvement of the whole congregation in the liturgy we now use, and for future revisions to be more imaginative in enabling this, especially in the eucharistic prayers. Parallel with the creative thinking that is needed centrally is creative local thinking: a local congregation might well be encouraged to produce its own rite, which could be a far more flexible liturgy than anything produced centrally, and really express the life and concerns of that particular community, while at the same time including in some form words and actions which are generally agreed to be essential to a eucharist. It may be that such 'experimental' forms are better suited to small groups than large congregations, at least to begin with; which leads on to the next question.

(ix) How should the practice be introduced locally?

I noted in the introduction that however obvious most of this booklet will seem to many of its readers, it will seem far from obvious to many of our regular faithful members; and there is usually representation of this traditionalism amongst lay leadership of nay church. The first thing that is needed is education: people need to know that a large portion of the Christian church always has welcomed children to communion, and that in the West, where the practice died out for reasons that are now discredited, there is increasing evidence of widespread revival of interest and practice. They need to know, as has been stated several times, that in almost half the dioceses in England 'authorized' experiments are under way (in Southwark this has been the case in many parishes for several years). They are likely, though not certain, to have experienced the presence of children at the eucharist, and they may have become sentimentally attached to the procedure of 'blessing' rather than communicating them.[1] It should be pointed out that this is an anomalous alternative, that it is wrong to make blessings a substitute for communion, that it is simply a temporary expedient which should not become a permanent practice. Congregations of an intellectual type will need to learn that a cerebral approach to communion is only partially valid, and needs to be accompanied by that sense of true participation of which children are just as capable as adults—if not more so. Congregations of a traditional type need to grasp the corporate nature of communion, and to be delivered from the type of individualism that finds children a distraction. At the same time it must be said that for parents of young children the occasional eucharist *without* their toddlers can still be a time of great refreshment! It has been well said that adults do not invite children to *all* their meals. So provided that family eucharist is the norm, the occasional (quieter?) adult eucharist, perhaps in the evening, might well meet a pastoral need. It could enable all of us with better grace to welcome children to communion!

(v) Is the church building really the place for young children?

At present, the answer in many cases may well be 'no'. *We* may be as welcoming as we like, but the building may not be. As with liturgy, we do not want to be dominated by considerations about children: but the participation of children may well demand some rethinking as to the building's suitability for the whole family of God. Something has already been said about letting children have a hand in the decoration of the church; but more fundamental changes are probably necessary. Chairs have a flexibility pews lack, and can be arranged to allow for movement: either planned movement as part of the worship, or spontaneous movement. Toddlers are going to be moving in any case, so let us not make life more difficult than it needs to be for them and for their parents. I can still remember the piercing shriek as my daughter fell in between one pew and the next in the middle of a rather lengthy eucharist. If the congregation are all together throughout, a carpeted 'quiet play' area can be very helpful during sermon, creed, notices etc.; but equally perhaps youngsters ought to be increasingly involved in each of these activities. A good P.A. system is essential, because

[1] There is still a case for 'blessing' children who are only occasionally in church.

although children have better hearing than their seniors, they are less tolerant of inaudibility or of invisibility, so that they and their families should be encouraged to set near the front, and the table should be sufficiently raised for the eucharistic actions to be clearly visible to all. The church must be warm enough for mothers to bring infants without anxiety, even in the severest weather. There should be good toilet facilities, with provision for nappy-changing. There must be parking room for prams and push-chairs. On a more profound level, it may be necessary to make alterations to the communion rail or wherever communion is received, so that children can kneel or stand without falling over or falling through; and it goes without saying that a long trek up countless steps to a high altar at the east end is undesirable. After the service, as adults drink their coffee and children have consumed their squash, it would be a bonus that on a fine day there was an area outside where they could play: I am not in favour of riotous behaviour inside church, any more than in our best room at home. A certain amount of mystery needs to be preserved, in the building as in the liturgy. But a final small point: is there some way of making our heavy church doors swing open at a child's touch: that would be symbolically satisfying!

(xi) Can tiny children manage bread and wine?

We may need to be somewhat more flexible in our distribution of the elements if we are going to welcome children to communion. For very tiny children only a very tiny morsel of bread slightly moistened with wine has any chance of being eaten, and we must be prepared for that to be placed in the child's mouth, if necessary more than once. But as soon as the child is old enough to reach out his hand for the bread and the cup, he should be given the bread in his hand, and allowed to sip from (but not necessarily hold!) the cup. It may be easier for the president to communicate one parent and then allow him or her to communicate the rest of the family; as parents, the adults will know of what their child is capable and how to make the distribution meaningful for him. Training is probably needed for this, and a generally more relaxed but still reverent approach to the elements. The type of bread and wine should be that which is best for the whole family of God: the bread should be of white flour and as light as possible in texture, possibly Danish style. Certainly it must not be doughy or chewy, and there must be *no crust:* presidents who enjoy rending apart the brittle carapace of a large bap probably have better teeth than the majority of their congregation and certainly do not have to sweep up the fragments that litter the sanctuary floor after they have gone![1] The wine should be ordinary communion wine, sweet and red: I see no reason to dilute it, unless that really is more palatable to the children—which I doubt, having seen my younger daughter at two sipping with obvious relish at a glass of cream sherry. It is a matter of the children being accustomed from an early age to share in the bread and wine, so that they become accustomed to it. If on any occasion they do not wish to partake, no fuss should be made. Nor should there be any anxiety about the words of distribution: I just do not believe that even a very young child who has been accustomed to hear the words

[1] Not that the difficulties of texture need drive us to the 'convenient', but unauthentic, wafer.

and receive the elements for as long as he or she can remember will be in any danger of thinking that there is ordinary blood in the cup. This is a matter of continuing nurture: but from an early age children understand symbolic language, and can actually play with words, switching back and forth from symbolic to literal in a way which shows they can both understand the distinction and also hold together symbolic and literal in their minds without becoming confused. Their understanding of the body of Christ and the blood of Christ must be linked to the bread and wine right from the start.

(xii) What should we do with the children before and after the distribution?

Assuming a large congregation, the distribution of communion will take some time, however well organized; and this has been in the past the source of some embarrassment for those with small children present. It is not the occasion (there usually is not one during Family Communion) for quiet devotional reflection by individuals; nor is it the moment (again, there should not be such a moment) for handing the toys to the kids in the vain hope that they will amuse themselves and not distract anyone else. I would suggest that well-known and not too boisterous songs and choruses should be sung throughout or for a good portion of the time, so that there is a focus for the whole congregation; in particular, enough of the children's attention will be held to keep them in tune with what is going on. Perhaps there might even be some dance or movement as people move to and from the rail. Certainly it is a time for keeping in touch with one another, the very last time at which we ought to be withdrawing into our own privatized spiritual climate. When there is no singing, quiet conversation about the appropriate picture book (see booklist) could be helpful; or individuals could take it in turn to say quiet but audible prayers from an agreed family source. There is nothing wrong with specific thanksgivings and intercessions at this point. If small children grow restless, I have already said that I think the layout of the church should permit a gentle wander round, preferably without parents feeling they have to follow; but I would make it a matter of discipline to prevent aggressive or disruptive games. Part of our ministry in all this will be to parents, since welcoming their children to communion will, as I know from personal experience, expose any weaknesses they may have in their discipline at home. Communion may well provide the firm but friendly framework from which they can learn parenting skills that will be valuable elsewhere.

(xiii) What about families moving to other parishes?

Those of us who have been struggling with baptismal discipline in our parishes will know how heartbreaking it is when our sensitive (as we hope) pastoral and evangelistic policy is undermined by neighbouring parishes (or free churches) who will baptize all-comers. We have longed for a diocesan and ecumenical policy, as in some Anglican provinces abroad. Some sort of wider policy will desperately be needed also, should the practice of welcoming children to communion continue to grow. In this mobile society, we are already encountering the problems of families whose children have been welcomed to communion in one parish, moving to another parish in which they are not. How can it be explained to them? What can parents do? Commute to the nearest church that *will* communicate their children? Defy the Vicar and communicate their children themselves? Suffer the situation and work hard to change it? But the latter course has at present little support at higher levels; and should one sacrifice one's own children in the struggle? The only answer that will meet the case is for Synod to grasp the nettle and declare: once a communicant, always a communicant. Local churches should not have the power to excommunicate, and especially not to excommunicate children. That might come under the Lord's strictures about not causing little ones to stumble. Once we have welcomed children to communion, we dare not exclude them again. It may be that within a parish which does not feel itself ready for a full implementation of the practice of infant communion there are groups who would be open to such a practice, in which case communion can be administered in these groups: but this must only be a temporary expedient, for it represents a division in the body of Christ which must be healed. I am not convinced that there are strong grounds on this issue for a conscience clause: the duty of our consciences in this case is mainly towards the children. I am labouring this point because I feel it to be pastorally so vital: if it is wrong to exclude baptized children from the eucharist in the first place, it is doubly wrong to exclude them once they have been made welcome elsewhere.

There is an ecumenical dimension to this problem also, especially in areas of local ecumenical projects, where churches are combined. Here I think one must trust that the Spirit is speaking to all the churches.[1] All that has been said, applies to any local congregation, whether just Anglican, or a mixture of Anglican, Methodist, U.R.C. etc. Certainly it would be an irrelevance to hold back from welcoming children to communion out of ecumenical timidity.

3. RESOURCES

I am allocating a fair proportion of this booklet to resources, because, having stated what I believe to be the general principles and the practical questions, I am aware that many people will want to follow up various points in far greater depth than a Grove booklet allows. But not wanting to appear coy, I am dealing with Grove Publications first!

News of Liturgy
those who subscribe to this stimulating broadsheet will have noticed the occasional entry relevant to this subject. Of special interest are:

Issue 80 (August 1981) in which are set out the New Zealand guidelines for the admission of children to communion and confirmation or laying-on-of-hands by bishop. There are no surprises here, but they combine moderation with flexibility in a commendable manner.

Issue 93 (September 1982) in which the editorial reflects on the general principle.

Issue 97 (January 1983) which documents the background to the (then) forthcoming synod motion, and also contains an hilarious plea (originating in that den of liturgical brigands in Nottingham) for the restoration of the ancient practice of infant ordination, under the auspices of IOCM (Infants Ordinands Council for Ministry). Better not show that to the PCC!

Issue 98 (February 1983) which contains a much truer assessment of Synod's reaction to the Winchester motion than did the *Church Times*.

Grove Books
These have been referred to at various points in the text, but to save endless footnotes I have reserved proper comment until now. (Ministry and) Worship series:

3. *Baptismal Discipline* by Colin Buchanan
5. *A Service of Thanksgiving and Blessing* by Christopher Byworth and John Simpson
8. *Communion, Confirmation, and Commitment* by Christopher Byworth
9. *Patterns of Sunday Worship* by Colin Buchanan—(valuable for a picture of the 'integrated' morning)
16. *Alternative Eucharistic Prayers* by D. Billings (creative possibilities)
20. *A Case for Infant Baptism* by Colin Buchanan.
69. *The Attractive Church* by Kenneth White
73. *Family Festivals:* (I must declare an interest, but note the use of the link versicle and response: Let us give thanks to the Lord our God/It is right to give him thanks and praise.)
77. *Intercessions in worship* by M. Vasey

At the time of writing nos. 3, 5, 7, 8, and 9 are out of print. Much of the thrust of these booklets is also to be found in Colin Buchanan, Trevor Lloyd, Harold Miller (eds.) *Anglican Worship Today: Collins Illustrated Guide to the Alternative Service Book 1980* (Collins, 1980).

Grove Liturgical Studies:

1. *Sacramental initiation complete in baptism:* by E. C. Whitaker. (This is now sadly out of print, but is unique as far as I know for its combination of accessibility and thoroughness. If enough people enquire . . . !)
27. *Infant Communion—Then and Now* by David Holeton. (Essential reading: an historical survey that focuses fascinatingly on certain periods in the history of the practice, and makes one aware of the shallowness of our theology and church life.)

Specific treatments comcerning the admission of children to communion.

'. . . and do not hinder them': an ecumenical plea for the admission of children to the eucharist.
This is perhaps the single most valuable recent publication on the subject. It is published by the World Council of Churches, and obtainable from the British Council of Churches, 2 Eaton Gate, London SW1W 9RQ.

It is a collection of essays together with the report of a consultation on the subject, and it presents a wide variety of perspectives, including those of the children themselves. It is particularly strong on ecclesiology, and contains a contribution from the Orthodox church, as well as an overview of what is happening denominationally by David Holeton.

Children at the Table and
Children and Holy Communion—time to say YES

These two related documents from the Church of Scotland are, respectively: a comprehensive symposium both theological and historical, and a report to the General Assembly in 1982 unsurpassed for the clarity of its presentation. These documents are obviously from a different perspective, in that eucharistic discipline has always been distinctive in the Church of Scotland; but they are nonetheless most valuable. Obtainable from the Department of Education, 121 George Street, Edinburgh EH2 4YN.

Crosscurrent no. 6

This issue of the excellent National Society journal was devoted entirely to the subject 'Children and the Eucharist' which is invaluable as giving access to reports of experiments in several different settings, with really practical details described. There is also a lengthy article by Prebendary John Fisher summarizing his views on confirmation. Nat. Soc., Church House, Dean's Yard, Westminster SW1P 3NZ.

The nature and nurture of children

The Child in the Church (B.C.C.). The famous report, which gives a history of Christian nurture, and develops along broad lines the paths we should be taking now. It contains numerous recommendations, among which is the admission of children to communion as part of their Christian nurture. It also calls for more theological work to be done: hence

Understanding Christian nurture: in which various themes relevant to children at communion are developed, and deeper insights pursued into the whole Christian nurture of children.

Not in front of the children by Ronald H. Green (Mowbrays). This is the outline of one of the early Southwark experiments which has been properly monitored and its great pastoral value assessed. It also contains guidelines for a syllabus to accompany the admission of twelve-year-olds to communion followed by confirmation two years later.

Take time to grow series (Post Green Press, 57 Dorchester Road, Lytchett Minster, Poole, Dorset, BH16 6JE): There are at present two publications in this series: *Beginnings,* and *Creation: Enjoy and Discover.* The first is a 10-14 week course for adults involved with children aged 0-5 years, an aid to helping children grow in the knowledge of God and for discovering together what it means for children and adults to be part of God's family. The second is for groups of children between the ages of 9 and 13. The course contains structured activity and worship on the theme of creation. It is divided into three parts: Part 1 is study material for teachers or leaders; part 2 is the course material for children and part three contains readings and music on the theme of creation for use in the worship times. Courses for other age groups are being developed.

Family worship and spirituality

Successful family devotions by Mary White (published by Navpress, U.S.A.).

Family Devotion Ideas Book: by E. Blitchington (Bethany House, U.S.A.).

Time for the family (Scripture Union Magazine): It is worth sending for the S.U. catalogue: 130 City Road, London EC1V 2NJ.

Benjamin Books: (Church Information Office, Dean's Yard): Picture books to stimulate conversation between adults and children on a wide variety of topics. It is worth sending for their catalogue, too.

Christian education for all ages within the parish

Live, learn and worship; This is the Life; Share the Word; All generations: all these are published by C.I.O., Church House, Dean's Yard, Westminster, and provide an exciting variety of integrated learning for the whole church. C.I.O. also do things for separate age groups.

Sunday Learning for all Ages by Judith Rose (Grove Pastoral Series no. 11, 1982). This is distinctively non-sacramental, but very thorough.

Four Celebrations: a four week teaching course set within the actual context of the Family Communion Service.

His Spirit is with us by Leslie Francis (Collins): comprehensive Christian nurture based on the eucharist.

Liturgy and learning through the life cycle by John Westerhoff and William H. Willimon (Seabury Press). This is an interesting, though at times rhetorical, essay in the application of liturgy as an instrument of nurture throughout the Christian life.

Liturgical/sacramental

Worship and the Child: essays by the Joint Liturgical Group (S.P.C.K.): rather overtaken by events, though worth getting for Neville Clarke's essays.

Family Services by Kenneth Stevenson (Alcuin/S.P.C.K.).

The Baptismal Liturgy by E. C. Whitaker (S.P.C.K.).

Confirmation then and now: J. D. C. Fisher (Alcuin/S.P.C.K.). This is the fullest current statement of the view that initiation should include the laying on of hands, from someone who *on those grounds* I detect would be happy to welcome children to communion.

Christian Initiation: Birth and Growth in the Christian Society (the 'Ely Report') (C.I.O.).

Bells are ringing by Brother Kenneth (C.I.O.): a take-to-church book for under-sevens, to help them understand Rite A.

The Lord is here (Collins): similar.

Roman Catholic material (all obtainable from Catholic Truth Society)

Directory on Children's masses
Constitution on the liturgy
General instruction on the Roman missal
Letter on eucharistic prayers
Eucharistic prayers for masses with children and masses of reconciliation

Other interesting liturgical evidence:

But that I can't believe! by J. A. T. Robinson (Fontana) pp.108-116: In the chapter entitled 'Local Liturgy', John Robinson makes a strong case for home-grown eucharists, giving as an example one devised at St. Mark's-in-the-Bowerie, New York.

Questioning Worship? by T. G. A. Baker (S.C.M.). He is asking sympathetic but penetrating questions of the revised liturgy, and in particular he works out possible guidelines for any parish wanting to construct its own eucharist. He was writing pre-ASB, and looked forward to it, but said that it should be accompanied by continuing liturgical creativity.

APPENDIX: SUGGESTED LITURGICAL MATERIAL FOR THE HOME

At breakfast before the family goes to communion.

Leader Jesus said to the apostles, 'I have wanted so much to eat this passover meal with you before I suffer . . .'. (Luke 22.15)

Let us give thanks to the Lord our God.

All **It is right to give him thanks and praise.**

Leader Most merciful Lord, we thank you for this special day when we and all your people remember how Jesus died for us. As we share bread and wine, may we also share in his new life.

At the midday meal following communion

Leader Jesus broke the bread and gave it to them. Then their eyes were opened and they recognized him . . . (Luke 24.30, 31).

Let us give thanks to the Lord our God.

All **It is right to give him thanks and praise.**

Leader We thank you, Lord, for making yourself know to us in what has been said and done this morning. May we and all your people make you known to others in what we say and do.

Alternatively, the Didache, a very early Christian document whose full (if pretentious) title is 'The teaching of the twelve apostles' contains the following marvellous prayer of thanksgiving following the eucharist:

> We give thanks to you, holy Father, for your holy name which you have enshrined in our hearts, and for the knowledge and faith and immortality which you have made known to us through your child, Jesus; glory to you for evermore.
>
> You, Lord Almighty, created all things for the sake of your name and gave food and drink to men for their enjoyment, that they might give you thanks; but to us you have granted spiritual food and drink for eternal life through your child Jesus. Above all, we give you thanks because you are mighty; glory to you for evermore. Amen.

Didache 10.2-4 (ed. Jasper & Cuming)

A proper preface which might be used when newly baptized people are to be welcomed to communion:

> And now we give you thanks for *X, Y, Z,* who by baptism have been buried with Christ and raised to the new life in which we share.
>
> Therefore with angels, *etc.* . . .